MW01070138

#ichooseme

Lisa V. Taitt-Stevenson

#ichooseme Copyright © 2022
by Lisa V. Taitt-Stevenson

All rights reserved.

All right reserved. No part of this book may be reproduced or used in any manner without the prior written permission of the copyright owner, except for the use of brief quotations in a book review.

The Everyday Life Bible: Notes & Commentary by Joyce Meyer. First Edition: Faith Words. New York, NY 2020. Print.
https://www.youversion.com/apps/New International Version
https://www.youversion.com/apps/New King James Version

Cover design by Chalimar Shree' LLC

Lisa V. Taitt-Stevenson
Visit my website at www.lisavtaittstevenson.org

Printed in the United States of America
First Printing: February 2022

LWI Publishing
Services

#ichooseme Copyright © 2022 by Lisa V. Taitt-Stevenson
All rights reserved.
ISBN: 978-1-7335255-7-2

DEDICATION

This book is dedicated to every woman that needs to be reminded that they do not need permission to choose themselves.

ACKNOWLEDGMENTS

I want to thank Gigi for being my test Goddess on this #ichooseme journey. Thank you for trusting me and believing in me.

Choosing you and knowing why you are choosing you is important. Oftentimes, we start planning our life's journey and are not able to complete that plan because we have not defined our "why." Your "why" will be the fuel behind what you do, how you do it, and if you accomplish what you set out to achieve.

You purchased this book with the intention to choose you, and we are going to ensure that your choice and your why remains consistent starting with a 30-day plan transitioning to a way of life.

Let's start by boldly, intentionally, and unapologetically declaring that you are worthy to be chosen!
Let that sink in for a minute...
YOU ARE WORTHY TO BE CHOSEN!

Now that we have stated the obvious...

Let's identify your "why." Why are you consciously choosing you? You must have a why. Your why is going to push you to choose you every day for the next 30 days and beyond. And if you don't know your why, I am going to help you figure it out:

Choose you because of that little girl that fought for you to stand here today.

Choose you every day because of every tear she wiped away.

Choose you for every piece of dirt she brushed off her knees.

Choose you because of every scar she endured (the ones you can see and the ones you cannot).

Choose you because regardless of every bruise she weathered and every pain she ingested, she kept getting up and pushing through.

Choose you because when you choose you, there is another woman that is watching you work through choosing you.

Choose you!

When you choose you, you will make sure that your decisions are based on your choice and not someone else's.

Choose you!

When you choose you, you are setting the temperature within the room. You will no longer be the thermometer but the thermostat.

Choose you!

You are worthy of that choice. You are deserving of that choice, from the crown of your head to the souls of your feet.

Choose you!

During your daily transformation, you will be choosing and acknowledging different parts of yourself. However, right now, at this very moment, as you get ready to start this journey, I want you to choose you... on purpose and with purpose!

Choose you!

Now let's get started!

Reminder

"Love yourself first"

Okay !

~Day 1~
Hello Beautiful

Proverbs 15:13-15, NLT: "A glad heart makes a happy face."

As women, we often utilize our smiles to hide our pain. There was a time I did not smile on the inside, even though I wore a smile on the outside.

Today I choose me

Today I choose me because I deserve to be chosen

Today I choose to see and acknowledge my smile

Today I choose to love my smile; The one that can light up any room I walk into

Today I choose to embrace the smile that fought to be here

Today I choose to recognize that when I smile others are inclined to smile along with me; My smile can brighten someone's day; My smile is powerful

Today I am going to take a moment to look in the mirror and take note that since I was made in GOD's image, I truly have my daddy's smile

Today I choose to no longer hide my smile

Today I am going to close my eyes and bask in the beauty and the impact of my smile

Today I will take the time to really feel the corners of my mouth rise into a big, beautiful smile

Today I will smile as I feel the joy of GOD's love filling me up to the brim

Today my smile will be intentional

Today I will choose to smile knowing that as I smile, GOD is smiling right along with me

Today I choose me

Today I choose me and my smile because we deserve to be chosen

#ichooseme

Write down a time that the smile on your face was truly a reflection of the joy you felt on the inside.
As you write, sit in that joyful moment and smile!
What beautiful things do you notice about your smile?

TODAY I CHOOSE ME BECAUSE:

~Day 2~
Hello Gorgeous

Proverbs 31:8-9, ESV: "Open your mouth for the mute, for the rights of all who are destitute. Open your mouth, judge righteously, defend the rights of the poor and needy."

There were times in my life when I did not recognize my voice. I had released ownership of my voice.

Today I choose me
Today I choose me because I deserve to be chosen
Today I choose to listen to and acknowledge my voice
Today I choose to hear my melodic tone as I say aloud: "I CHOOSE ME!!!"
Today I choose to listen to the color of my voice; The power in my voice; The humility in my voice
Today I choose to hear The GOD in my voice; The voice that is music to GOD's ears
Today I choose to recognize my voice; The voice that calms a storm; The voice that can motivate a nation
Today I choose to ensure my voice is laced with love; A love that no one could deny even if they tried
Today I choose to listen to the voice that gives power to the words that can speak life or death
Today I choose my voice to be as big as a mountain or as small as a pebble
Today I choose to use my voice to teach or preach
Today I choose my voice to spread a word or The Word
Today I choose to listen to the voice that is unmistakably mine
Today I choose to use my beautifully melodic voice to choose me because me and my voice deserve to be chosen
#ichooseme

What do you notice about your voice? What do you use your voice for? How often do you use your voice for you?

TODAY I CHOOSE ME BECAUSE:

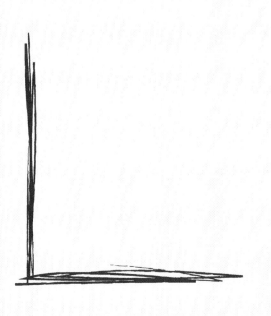

~Day 3~
Hello Queen

Psalm 62:5-7, NKJV: "My soul, wait silently for GOD alone, for my expectation is from Him. He only is my rock and my salvation; He is my defense; I shall not be moved. In GOD is my salvation and my glory; The rock of my strength, And my refuge, is in GOD"

My soul has been tired. I felt defenseless and lost from within.

Today I choose me
Today I choose me because I deserve to be chosen
Today I choose to remember to find rest
Today I choose to rest in the fact that I was born chosen
Today I choose to rest, reassured that when God created me, He was pleased
Today I choose to take a moment to rest and breathe as I say
"I choose me"
Today I choose to rest in those words
Today I choose to rest in the arms of the One that chooses me daily
Today I choose to rest my mind, my movements, and my thoughts
Today I choose to take a moment to breathe and focus solely on me
Today I choose to rest from the distractions from everything and everyone that wants me to choose them over me
Today I choose to rest and choose me in this space of rest
Today I am going to choose my space and place of rest
Today I choose me because I deserve to be chosen
#ichooseme

What will you intentionally choose to find rest in today? Is it difficult for you to rest? Is it difficult for you to find rest in resting? Why do you think that is?

TODAY I CHOOSE ME BECAUSE:

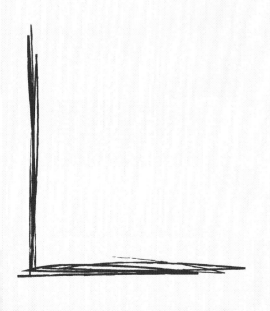

~Day 4 ~
Hello Woman of God

Psalm 139:13-16, MSG: "Oh yes, you shaped me first inside, then out; you formed me in my mother's womb. I thank you, High GOD—you're breathtaking! Body and soul, I am marvelously made! I worship in adoration— what a creation! You know me inside and out, you know every bone in my body; You know exactly how I was made, bit by bit, how I was sculpted from nothing into something. Like an open book, you watched me grow from conception to birth; all the stages of my life were spread out before you, the days of my life all prepared before I'd even lived one day."

There were parts of me that I did not love. I could not see how wonderfully I was made.

Today I choose me
Today I choose me because I deserve to be chosen
Today I choose to acknowledge the parts of me that I tried to ignore
Today I choose to look under the rug and behind the curtain
Today I choose to love the parts of me that I pray no one sees
Today I am choosing the parts of me that I tried to pray away
Today I choose to love the parts of me that I have convinced myself were not worthy to be chosen; the parts of me that I had chosen to devalue
Today I choose me because EVERY part of me has increasing value
Today I choose to shout, "I am worthy!"
Today I choose to love me beyond the scars that I can see and the ones I cannot; My scars do not decrease my value or my beauty; My visible and invisible scars show me that whatever "it" was "it" did not defeat me
Today I choose the part of my heart that I often think is too soft and too giving
Today I choose to see that is the heart that mimics Christ the most
Today I choose the parts of me that I allowed myself to believe were unlovable
Today I choose to see that without those parts, I would not be the me that I have been choosing these past few days, giving me my "why"
Today I intentionally choose to lovingly look at myself and say, "I choose me!"
I am going to take the time to acknowledge those beautiful parts of me separately
Today I am going to choose them, embrace them, love on them
Today I choose every part of me because EVERY part of me deserves to be chosen
#ichooseme

List the parts of you that you will no longer ignore or try to hide. Explain why you will no longer ignore those parts of you. Acknowledge each of them by lovingly and boldly choosing them in writing and out loud.

TODAY I CHOOSE ME BECAUSE:

~Day 5~
Hello Blessed One

Proverbs 15:4, AMP: "A soothing tongue [speaking words that build up and encourage] is a tree of life, but a perverse tongue [speaking words that overwhelm and depress] crushes the spirit."

Words mean something. I used to allow others' words to determine who I was and to speak over my life.

Today I choose me
Today I choose me because I deserve to be chosen
Today I choose to see and acknowledge my words
Today I choose to see that the words I use are in line with me choosing me
Today I choose to love myself aloud
Today I will let the words of love and admiration for me flow freely and unapologetically
Today I choose to ensure that my words speak life into me
Today I choose for my words to speak blessings
Today I choose for my words to speak victory
Today I choose to ensure that my words set the tone on how I expect to be spoken to
Today I choose to declare I am love, I am loved, I am light, I am chosen because I am worthy to be chosen
Today I choose to recognize I am beautiful, I am a child of the Most High, I am a part of the royal family
Today I choose to remind myself of ALL that I am in Christ; of ALL that God created me to be
Today I choose to whisper sweet nothings to the one that deserves these words the most...ME!!!
Today I choose to look in the mirror and say aloud: "I choose me!"
Today I choose me and my words because me and my words deserve to be chosen!
#ichooseme

Make 2 columns. Write in column A - What you used to say to yourself and about yourself. Write in column B – What you will now say to yourself and about yourself.

TODAY I CHOOSE ME BECAUSE:

~Day 6~
Hello God's Likeness

Psalms 51:10-12, NKJV: "Create in me a clean heart, O God, And renew a steadfast spirit within me. Do not cast me away from Your presence, And do not take Your Holy Spirit from me. Restore me to the joy of Your salvation."

There are moments when my thoughts are not pure. At times I feel removed from HIS presence.

Today I choose me
Today I choose me because I deserve to be chosen
Today I choose my thoughts
The ones that follow my words
The ones that cosign the words that speak to the virtuous woman that I am
Today I choose the thoughts that feed my soul but starve my haters, my doubters, my enemies
Today I choose the thoughts that remind me to say "won't" instead of "can't," for the things not best for me
Today I choose the thoughts that remind me to say no to what is not meant for me so I can say yes to me
Today I choose the thoughts that remind me to say no to my chaos so I can say yes to my peace
Today I choose the thoughts that remind me to say no to fear, guilt, and shame
Today I choose the thoughts that remind me to say no to lies, and yes to truth
Today I choose the thoughts that remind me that I am allowed to say no without explanation
Today I choose the thoughts that remind me as I wake every day to say, I choose me!
Today I choose my thoughts so that my thoughts will choose me
Today I choose me
Today I choose me because I deserve to be chosen
#ichooseme

There are some thoughts that have taken up residency in your mind and have overstayed their visit. Some of these thoughts were given to you but were not meant for you nor were they yours to keep. What are some of the thoughts that you are going to release today?

TODAY I CHOOSE ME BECAUSE:

~Day 7~
Hello God's Daughter

2 Corinthians 12:8-10, AMP: "Concerning this I pleaded with the Lord three times that it might leave me; but HE has said to me, "My grace is sufficient for you [My lovingkindness and My mercy are more than enough - always available - regardless of the situation]; for [My] power is being perfected [and is completed and shows itself more effectively] in [your] weakness." Therefore, I will all the more gladly boast in my weaknesses, so that the power of Christ [may completely enfold me and] may dwell in me. So I am well pleased with weaknesses, with insults, with distresses, with persecutions, and with difficulties, for the sake of Christ [for when I am weak [in human strength], then I am strong [truly able, truly powerful, truly drawing from GOD's strength]."

There are days where I struggle believing I should choose me. I feel unworthy of choosing me.

Today I choose me
Today I choose me because I deserve to be chosen
Today I choose me because sometimes as women, we move in with a significant other in order to be chosen; We may dress to be chosen; we may speak to be chosen; we may work to be chosen; we even trip and stumble because we are focused on the goal of being chosen by everyone else
Today I choose to acknowledge and declare that I have already been chosen by God
Today I choose to recognize I may I need to hear aloud that I have been chosen; I may need to hear someone say "I choose you"
Today I choose to hear my voice say aloud: "I choose me"
Today I choose to get in front of the mirror, look myself square in the eye, throw my shoulders back, and say it!
Today I choose to say it with love. I choose to say it with boldness
Today I am going to repeat it until I mean it
I choose me -> Say it again
I choose ME -> Say it again
I CHOOSE me -> Say it again
I CHOOSE ME!!!
Do you feel that? Do you feel what is happening? Do you feel the shift?
Walk in that bold and unapologetic choice, YOUR choice, to choose YOU
Today I choose me
Today I choose me because I deserve to be chosen
#ichooseme

In what ways are you going to choose and acknowledge you today?
But by the [remarkable] grace of God I am what I am, and
His grace toward me was not without effect....

TODAY I CHOOSE ME BECAUSE:

~Day 8~
Hello My Sister in Christ

Deuteronomy 32:10-11 (MSG) [replace "him"/ "them" with "me", and "its" with "my"] - "HE found him out in the wilderness, in an empty, windswept wasteland. HE threw his arms around him, lavished attention on him, guarding him as the apple of HIS eye. HE was like an eagle hovering over its nest, overshadowing its young, then spreading its wings, lifting them into the air, teaching them to fly...."

There are times when I am scared to spread my wings.

Today I choose me
Today I choose me because I deserve to be chosen
Today I choose to focus on my wings
Today I choose the ones GOD gave me so I can fly; the ones HE gave me to remind me that I am not to remain in this nest for too long
Today I choose to recognize every nest is a space to prepare and position me for my next space and place HE has created for me...all for HIS glory
Today I choose to realize the times I was uncomfortable, GOD was perhaps nudging me along and preparing me to take flight
Today I choose to accept that the times I was angry my place of "comfort" was no more, GOD was saying that it was time to get out of the nest and fly
Today I choose to be grateful that the times I was frustrated when the nest I was in was not "fitting" right no matter how hard I tried to make it work, GOD was saying, that nest was not for you anyway
Today I choose to acknowledge the wings that were created by HIM just for me
Today I choose to acknowledge that as I learn to spread my wings and fly as GOD intended, HE will be with me every step of the way
I choose to acknowledge my wings as they spread, and the wind (GOD's breath) helps me take flight and I begin to soar.
Today I choose me
Today I choose me because I deserve to be chosen
#ichooseme

When was there a time that GOD was moving you out of the nest for your own good? How did you feel? Were you afraid? Did you move willingly? Consider how GOD showed up for you in that situation. Now consider, if HE did it for you then, HE will do it for you now. Write your affirmation and confirmation.

TODAY I CHOOSE ME BECAUSE:

~Day 9~
Hello Chosen One

Philippians 4:13 (AMP) - "I can do all things [which He has called me to do] through Him who strengthens and empowers me [to fulfill His purpose—I am self-sufficient in Christ's sufficiency; I am ready for anything and equal to anything through Him who infuses me with inner strength and confident peace.]"

There are moments when I forget where my strength comes from.

Today I choose me
Today I choose me because I deserve to be chosen
Today I choose to believe that when I choose HIM, I choose me
Today I choose to see the part of me that most choose not to see
Today I choose to see the parts of me that I choose to lessen or downplay in order to allow others to "shine"
Today I choose to see the power within me; The power in me that makes the enemy flee; The same power that gave Moses the ability to part the Red Sea
Today I choose to see the power that resides in me; The power in me that allows me to not dwell on my current unclear vision of me Today I choose to focus on what I see, how HE sees me
Today I choose to celebrate the power in me
Today I choose to reside in the power in me
Today I choose to rest in the power in me
Today I choose to find solace in the power in me
Today I choose to declare my peace in the power in me
Today I choose me
Today I choose me because I deserve to be chosen
#ichooseme

Have you ever hidden a part of you for so long that you almost forgot it was there? What powerful part of you do you choose to see and acknowledge that the world doesn't? Why? Hiding the powerful parts of you doesn't benefit you nor anyone else.

TODAY I CHOOSE ME BECAUSE:

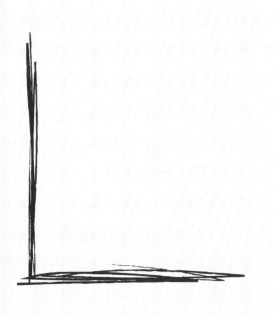

~Day 10~
Hello Virtuous Woman

1 Corinthians 3:16 (NIV): "Don't you know that you yourselves are God's temple and that God's Spirit dwells in your midst?"
Ephesians 2:10 (NIV): "For we are God's handiwork, created in Christ Jesus to do good works, which God prepared in advance for us to do."

There are days when I am not in love with this temple. There are moments when I do not respect this temple.

Today I choose me
Today I choose me because I deserve to be chosen
Today I choose to ask GOD to help me see me through HIS eyes
Today I choose to remember that I am fearfully and wonderfully made
Today I choose to remember that HE chose to carry HIS cross for me
Today I choose to see the me that HE chose to die for
Today I choose to respect the me that HE chose to be one of HIS own
Today I choose to see me through HIS eyes and no one else's
Today I choose to see that I am made in HIS image
Today I choose to see that it is HIS DNA that resides in me; HE breathed life in me
Today I choose to see that every day I wake is another day HE chose to have me here among the land of the living
Today I choose to see that I am an essential part of the body of Christ
Today I choose to read 1 Corinthians 12:4-26 to understand my value in the body of Christ
Today I choose me because GOD said I am worthy to be chosen
#ichooseme

How do you think GOD sees you? If you are not sure, spend time with HIM and ask HIM. Be intentional in your conversation. Recognize if you are going to ask, you must be willing to be patient and listen when HE answers.

TODAY I CHOOSE ME BECAUSE:

~Day 11~
Hello Beautiful

Proverbs 4:23 (NIV): "Above all else, guard your heart, for everything you do flows from it."

There were times when I chose others' thoughts and feelings and did not guard my heart.

Today I choose me
Today I choose me because I deserve to be chosen
Today I choose to see my heart
Today I choose the heart that was created, molded, and shaped by GOD himself for me
Today I choose the heart that God gave me to love the unlovable; the heart GOD provided me to love even when it is not returned; the heart that allows me to nurture others even from a space of exhaustion
Today I choose to see my heart that God looks at daily and says, "I am pleased!"
Today I choose the heart that is so strong it cannot be broken, and I will find the ability to love again
Today I choose my heart, which is so complex, and yet the amount of love it holds for Christ is incomprehensible
Today I choose to intentionally place my hand over my heart and feel my heartbeat; feeling the rhythm that was made just for me
Today I choose my heart's rhythm that is like no other; a heartbeat from the heart that provides:
Healing
Energy
Authenticity
Righteousness
Truth
Today I choose to see my heart; a heart that works just as hard for me as it does for everyone else
Today I choose me
Today I choose me because I deserve to be chosen
#ichooseme

How would you describe your heart? How is your heart like Christ's heart?

TODAY I CHOOSE ME BECAUSE:

~Day 12~
Hello Gorgeous

Isaiah 41:10 (NIV) - "So do not fear, for I am with you; do not be dismayed, for I am your God. I will strengthen you and help you; I will uphold you with my righteous right hand."

There are moments where the storms in my life have overtaken me.

Today I choose me
Today I choose me because I deserve to be chosen
Today I choose to see my storms; the storms GOD allowed me to weather
Today I choose to rejoice in the storms that did not break me; the storms that strengthened me; the storms that guided me; removed things from me; added things to me
Today I choose to acknowledge the storms that tried to take me out but failed miserably
Today I choose to see my "umbrella" as I am looking at my storms
Today I choose to praise My protector and provider in those storms
Today I choose to see the me that was standing in those storms
Today I choose to respect the resilient me; the me made in His image; the me who NEVER went through those storms alone
Today I choose to remember who was piloting my plane when there was turbulence
Today I choose to remember who was always in the boat with me when the waves were crashing
Today I choose to be reminded of I am reminded of who controls the winds in my life
Today I choose to give honor to the One who gives me the ability to see me
Today I choose to see me; the blessed and fortunate me He chose to endure these storms; just as Jesus chose to endure the ultimate storm for me
Today I choose me; because He chose me, which reminds me that I deserve to be chosen
Today I choose me
#ichooseme

Today I challenge you to write down a specific storm that as you were going through it, you didn't know if or how you would make it through. But as you reflect on it now, you see that God was there every step of the way, and you see what was gained or removed.

TODAY I CHOOSE ME BECAUSE:

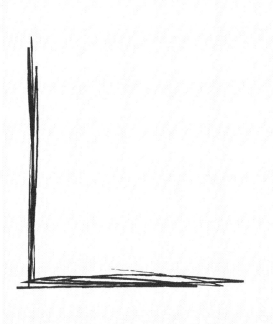

~Day 13~
Hello Queen

Matthew 6:12 (AMP): "And forgive us our debts, as we have forgiven our debtors [letting go of both the wrong and the resentment]." Psalm 32:1 (AMP): "Blessed [fortunate, prosperous, favored by God] is he whose transgression is forgiven, and whose sin is covered." Romans 8:1 (NIV): "Therefore, there is now no condemnation for those who are in Christ Jesus"

I have been forgiving others and unforgiving towards me.

Today I choose me
Today I choose me because I deserve to be chosen
Today I choose to see the forgiven me not the condemned me
Today I choose to see the me that was resurrected with Christ and born again
Today I choose the me that was placed here to witness and not to judge
Today I choose the me that is not defined by my sins, but by:
My destiny
My greatness
My heart
Who I am in Christ
Today I choose me by what GOD has declared for me
Today I choose me by who GOD calls me:
Beloved - 1 John 3:1
Blessed - Matthew 5:3-12
Faithful - Hebrews 11:6
Righteous - 2 Corinthians 5:21
Daughter - 2 Corinthians 6:17,18
Salt - Matthew 5:13(a)
Anointed - 1 John 2:27
Bride - Revelation 21:2
Today I choose me
Today I choose all of me because every part of me was defined and chosen by HIM
#ichooseme

Forgiveness is a Christ requirement. Forgiveness can be difficult, but we have the Holy Spirit with us to help us in that space. Forgiveness is also a reflection of you choosing you. As you forgive, you become free from the weight of unforgiveness. When choosing people to forgive, have you chosen to forgive yourself? If not, what's holding you back? The same forgiveness others deserve from you is the same forgiveness you deserve from yourself.

TODAY I CHOOSE ME BECAUSE:

~Day 14~
Hello Woman of God

Exodus 4:2(a), KJV: "Then the Lord said to him, "What is that in your hand""

There are days when I feel I am not prepared for the moment.

Today I choose me
Today I choose me because I deserve to be chosen
Today I choose to look at what is in my hand
Today I choose to see what God has already placed on the inside of me
Today I choose to be like Moses and look at what is in my hand
Today I choose to see that my hands are tools used:
To bless
To provide value
To enhance
To protect
To heal
To encourage
To teach
To instruct
To love
Today I choose to see that when I am facing any challenge, issue, or obstacle, GOD is saying, "What do you have in your hand?"
Today I choose to recognize I knew this space and time was coming and HE has already equipped me
Today I choose to respond: "He built me for this"
Today I choose to accept I was prepared for a time such as this
Today I choose to look at my hands and see them the way God intended
Today I choose me, ALL of me because ALL of me deserves to be chosen
#ichooseme

When you take the time to choose yourself, you are saying, "I love myself". At this moment, how will you choose you? I challenge you today to read 1 Corinthians 13:4-8 and dare you to love yourself the way God instructed. Love yourself with patience and kindness... Write down how you will choose you today.

When the Lord said to Moses, "What is that in your hand", what was HE saying? HE was essentially saying, as you face this "obstacle" rather than looking around at "everyone and everything" else, rather than look at me and worry, look at what is already in your hand. Look at what I have placed on the inside of you. Look at the fact that I have already equipped you with what you need.

TODAY I CHOOSE ME BECAUSE:

~Day 15~
Hello Blessed One

Hebrews 11:1,2, KJV: "Now faith is the substance of things hoped for, the evidence of things not seen. For by it the elders obtained a good report"

There are days when I need to pull my strength from women in the Bible.

Today I choose me
Today I choose me because I deserve to be chosen
Today I choose to see me in God's Word
Today I choose to see where I am represented throughout His Word
Today I choose to see the Esther in me that was created for a time such as this
Today I choose to see the Sarah in me who reminds me that if God gave a Word to me, it WILL come to pass
Today I choose to see the Martha in me that can at times get caught up in the busyness of the day, and even in the midst of my busyness Jesus never takes His eyes off of me
Today I choose to see the Mary in me that sits at His feet waiting patiently for His word
Today I choose to see the woman who touched the hem of his garment in me for I am healed by my faith, and I am no longer hemorrhaging
Today I choose to see Noah's wife in me as I have been tasked to plant seeds that will grow remarkable things
Today I choose to see the Rahab in me because I am a woman of strong courage and I have a strong devotion to my family
Today I choose to see the Miriam in me because I am a protector
Today I choose to see Abigail in me because I am a woman who is wise, decisive, and sensitive. I am a woman whose strengths are seen and recognized by those I meet.
Today I choose to see that I am the women in the bible, and they are me
Today I choose to see that I was chosen then, and I am chosen now
Today I choose me
Today I choose every part of me and every woman in me because WE deserve to be chosen
#ichooseme

Which Bible character resonates with you today? How will you use their testimony to choose you today?

TODAY I CHOOSE ME BECAUSE:

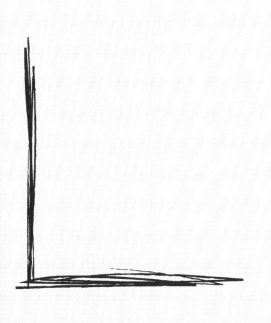

~Day 16~
Hello God's Likeness

Proverbs 4:26 (ESV): "Ponder the path of your feet; then all your ways will be sure."

At times, my feet are unsure of which direction I should go.

Today I choose me
Today I choose me because I deserve to be chosen
Today I choose to see my feet; the feet that move when needed
Today I choose the feet that carry me from here to there
Today I choose the feet that carry me along with whatever else I am carrying
Today I choose to pamper my feet
Today I choose to acknowledge my feet
Today I choose to love on my feet; my exhausted, hurt feet despite all they are feeling at any given moment
Today I choose the feet I cram into shoes
Today I choose the feet I subject to sand too hot or water too cold
Today I choose the feet that have yet to fail me
Today I choose the feet that remind me my steps are ordered
Today I choose to see my feet; the ones that look just like the ones Jesus washed; the feet that even Jesus did not discount
Today I choose the feet that remind me that I am walking in the history of my victory
Today I choose to see my feet
Today I choose to see that there is NO part of me that should not be chosen
Today I choose EVERY part of me because EVERY part of me deserves to be chosen
#ichooseme

Have you taken care of your feet today? Have you pampered your feet?
What direction has your feet moved for you to choose you? Are your
feet ready as in Ephesians 6:15?

TODAY I CHOOSE ME BECAUSE:

~Day 17~
Hello God's Daughter

Deuteronomy 30: 19(b), 20(a) (ESV): "Therefore choose life, that you and your offspring may live, loving the LORD your GOD, obeying his voice and holding fast to him, for he is your life and length of days..."

I haven't always believed I deserved a chance in life or at life beyond this life.

Today I choose me
Today I choose me because I deserve to be chosen
Today I choose to see the choice and the chance within me and around me
Today I choose to see that every day I have a choice and a chance to choose me
Today I choose to recognize the chance to choose how I am going to love me
Today I choose to acknowledge my choice with what I will receive and what I won't
Today I choose to take the chance to converse with my creator who is the only one who can define me
Today I choose to take a chance that is mine
Today I choose to take a chance to choose "and" over "or"
Today I choose to take a chance to choose freely what is best for me
Today I choose to believe in a chance to choose how I am going to live my life
Today I choose to take a chance to try and try again
Today I choose to accept the chance to let it go if I didn't get it "right" yesterday and start over again today
Today I choose to accept a chance at forgiveness
Today I choose to take a chance at happiness
Today I choose to seek a chance at abundance
Today I choose a chance at the life I desire
Today I choose a chance at life everlasting
Today I choose me
Today I choose to take advantage of the choice and chance to choose me daily because I deserve to be chosen
#ichooseme

No matter what happens in your life, you deserve a chance. This chance shouldn't be taken lightly or exhausted. What chance do you plan on giving yourself today?

TODAY I CHOOSE ME BECAUSE:

~Day 18~
Hello My Sister in Christ

Galatians 5:1, (AMP): "It was for this freedom that Christ set us free [completely liberating us]; therefore, keep standing firm and do not be subject again to a yoke of slavery [which you once removed]

I have felt locked up from within. Do I deserve to be free? If so, what am I to be free from?

Today I choose me
Today I choose me because I deserve to be chosen
Today I choose to see the freedom in me
Today I choose to understand that in order to fully see me I need to be free, free from the things that "hinder" me
Today I choose to be free from the things that skew my view of me
Today I choose freedom from the things that God did not create for me
Today I choose freedom from things that have overstayed their welcome within me; those things that have pushed past their season with me
Today I choose to discard things that never belonged to me
Today I choose to see the freedom within me
Today I choose to see the freedom to let go of my bags and finally, fully and intentionally leave ALL of them at the throne
Today I choose to see the freedom from condemnation
Today I choose to see the freedom from fear so I will push past my comfort zone and go for it because on the side of my comfort zone is my victory
Today I choose to see the freedom from worry; He said, "Cast your cares," and I will
Today I choose to see the freedom from my sins, yes even the ones I pray no one knows about and the ones I have yet to commit
Today I choose to see the freedom that choosing gives to me
Today I choose the freedom to dream far and wide
Today I choose the freedom to:
Laugh, love, shine and slay
Today I choose the freedom to be me
Today I choose freedom to realize that selflessness may require selfishness
Today I choose the freedom to see past what everyone else wants me to see and see what God has placed before me
Today I choose the freedom to be what God intended for me
Today I have the freedom to be what God created me to be
Today I recall that my freedom is based on who Jesus died for me to be
Today I choose to see the freedom in me
Today I freely choose me because I deserve to be chosen
#ichooseme

What bondage are you escaping from today? How will you choose to be free?

TODAY I CHOOSE ME BECAUSE:

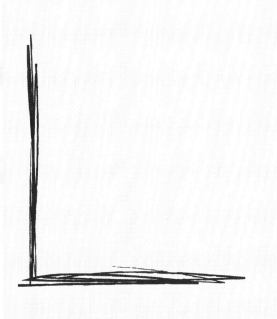

~Day 19~
Hello Chosen One

Matthew 5:37(a) (KJV): "But let your 'Yes' be 'Yes', and your 'No', 'No'."

When I know to say "No, I still say "Yes."

Today I choose me
Today I choose me because I deserve to be chosen
Today I choose to see the NO in me
Today I choose to use No as a complete sentence that deserves no explanation if I choose not to give one
Today I choose to see that a No to them could be a Yes to me
Today I choose to see that a No to something less than means I deserve more
Today I choose to accept that a No to crumbs reminds me I deserve a feast because my Father said a feast is being prepared for me, so I deserve no less
Today I choose not to be 2nd place because I was created to be first
Today I choose to no longer stand on 2nd place platforms expecting 1st place treatment
Today I choose to respond No to life's two-step because I deserve a waltz
Today I choose to say No to any "cubic zirconia" because I am a Diamond
Today I choose to see a No to a need to be pre-approved because I have already been approved by the only One that could approve me
Today I choose to see the NO within me needs to be the NO that comes out of me
So today I choose me when I say NO:
No more hurt; No more pain
No more leftovers; No more tears
No more doubt; No more shame
No more guilt; No, No, No
Today I choose to focus on the No's I can control, and the one's I cannot, I will rely on my Father to handle
Today I choose to embrace what I was created for:
Abundance and joy
Love and victory
Today I choose to get those things that I was gifted with the ability to have by boldly, courageously, unapologetically saying NO
Today I choose me
Today I choose to say NO to everyone and everything that wants me to choose them over me
Today I choose to say No to them and yes to me because I deserve to be chosen
#ichooseme

Where have you said Yes in your life when there should've been a No? How do you plan to take back your choice to say No?

TODAY I CHOOSE ME BECAUSE:

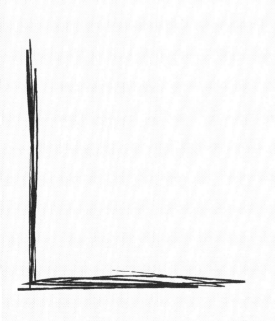

~Day 20~
Hello Virtuous Woman

Ephesians 1:3-4 (NLT): "*All praise to God, the Father of our Lord Jesus Christ, who has blessed us with every spiritual blessing in the heavenly realms because we are united with Christ. Even before he made the world, God loved us and chose us in Christ to be holy and without fault in his eyes.*"

Today I woke up tired. I was almost too tired to choose anything, including me. I barely wanted to get out of bed today.

Today I will rest in the fact that I am chosen
Today I am chosen by me
Today I am chosen by GOD
Today I choose me because I have already been validated
Today I choose me because I am valued
Today I choose me because I revere me
Today I choose me without hesitation or persuasion
Today I choose me without wondering if I am making the right choice
Today I choose to rest in the undeniable fact that I am worthy to be chosen
Today I choose to rest in the fact that every day I wake is a statement that I have already been chosen by HIM
Today as I choose me, I am boldly saying "I second the motion," and when Jesus asks, "All in favor?" all the angels proudly proclaim "Aye!"
Today I choose to see that the choice is me
The choice is me
The choice is me
I CHOOSE ME!!
Today when I decide to choose them (my fellow sisters), I will pause to ensure I am, in fact, choosing me, but if choosing "them" is a reflection of me not choosing me, then I must choose differently
Today I choose to recognize yesterday is gone; that choice was made
Today stands eagerly awaiting my decision
Today I choose to declare and decree that I Choose Me
Today I choose me
Today I choose me because I deserve to be chosen
#ichooseme

Today I choose me. How could I not choose me? I was created by Thee and HE resides in me. He is the reason I am Royalty. Write how and why you are worth choosing you.

TODAY I CHOOSE ME BECAUSE:

~Day 21~
Hello Beautiful

Proverbs 23:7(a) (KJV): "For as he (she) thinketh in his (her) heart, so is he (she):"

I woke up and it felt as if my thoughts were trying to deceive me. I am lost within my thoughts.

Today I choose me
Today I choose me because I deserve to be chosen
Today I choose to see my thoughts, even the ones that deceive me at times
Today I choose to fight the thoughts that regardless of what my mouth says, I don't even believe
Today I choose to see that my thoughts, my words, and my actions must be co-stars and aligned with one another
Today when I choose me, my actions and thoughts will operate with that choice
Today I choose to see some of my thoughts were on vacation long enough and now it is time for them to work
Today I choose to force my thoughts to choose me as well
Today I choose to see that when my thoughts run wild, I have the ability to reign them back in
Today I choose to SEE my thoughts and remove the ones that do me no good nor serve me any purpose and are not choosing me
Today I choose to see that some of these thoughts were mine and now I say, "you've taken up residency long enough, it's time to go!"
Today I choose to acknowledge the thoughts that were given to me; for the ones that were whispered to me oh so softly, I say, "go back to your owner, you don't belong here!"
Today I choose me, and it is time for my thoughts to choose me as well because I deserve to be chosen
#ichooseme

Your thoughts can be your saving grace or lead you to destruction. How will you align your thoughts so that you are now choosing you?

TODAY I CHOOSE ME BECAUSE:

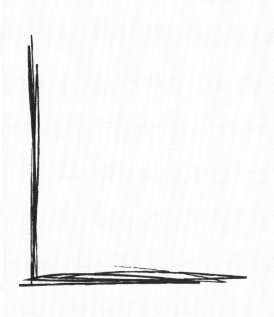

~Day 22~
Hello Gorgeous

Romans 8:28 (KJV): "And we know that all things work together for good to them that love God, to them who are called according to his purpose."

I woke up not feeling so beautiful. I feel a cloudy day coming.

Today I choose me
Today I choose me because I deserve to be chosen
Today I choose to see my flaws, my missteps, my storms, my hiccups
Today I choose to embrace all the things that contributed to the beautiful woman that I am today
Today I celebrate
The storms that strengthened me
The storms I rode out for another
The missteps that awakened me
The winds that removed things from me
The downpours that added valuable things to me
The failures that taught me
The flaws that made Jesus choose me when He came for the "broken", not the "righteous"
The lessons that matured me
The valleys that reminded me I was stronger than I thought
The heartaches that showed me I was blessed to have loved
The tears that showed my compassion and empathy
The pitfalls that strengthened my faith
Today I choose to see my flaws, my missteps, my storms, my hiccups
Today I choose me because I deserve to be chosen
#ichooseme

Talk about a flaw, misstep, storm, hiccup that while in it, it seemed as if it were against you but now as you are on this journey of choosing you, you see where it was necessary/needed; how it added value; how it served a purpose. What did you learn from it?

TODAY I CHOOSE ME BECAUSE:

~Day 23~
Hello Queen

Philippians 4:13 (KJV): "I can do all things through Christ which strengtheneth me"

There are moments where I need to be reminded where my strength comes from.

Today I choose me
Today I choose me because I deserve to be chosen
Today I choose to see my flexibility, resilience, strength, perseverance, breakthroughs, and victories
Today I choose to see, all that tried to take me down did not succeed
Today I choose to see how I may have bent this way and that way, but I was never broken
Today I choose to recall how at times I questioned God's belief that I could handle all that was given to me
Today I choose to see, I could, and I can
Today I choose to see my flexibility, resilience, strength, perseverance, breakthroughs, and victories because of who resides in me
Today I choose to see the David in me, realizing that when armed with a "mere stone" and slingshot I can take down my giants; not necessarily because of the stone and slingshot, but because of the God who covers me
Today I choose to see the Noah in me where my obedience brought me my victory
Today I choose to see that my Jericho walls don't' stand a chance against me
Today I choose to see the Meshach, Shadrach, and Abednego in me; even though I may walk through the fire or have been thrown into the flames, I will come out unscathed and not smelling like smoke
Today I choose to see that at times "life" may come at me, at times "life" may not choose me, but what remains unchanged, unaltered, unwavering is that I choose me
Today I choose to see my flexibility, resilience, strength, perseverance, breakthroughs, and victories
I choose to see me because I deserve to be chosen
#ichooseme

List some of your flexibility, resilience, strength, perseverance, breakthroughs, and victories that you choose to see today. Rest in those things. Acknowledge who you were and who you are now in them.

TODAY I CHOOSE ME BECAUSE:

~Day 24~
Hello Woman of God

Mark 12:31 (KJV): "The second is this: 'Love your neighbor as yourself.' There is no commandment greater than these."

Today I recognize I give so much of myself to others that I leave less for me.

Today I choose me
Today I choose me because I deserve to be chosen
Today I choose to see the liberties in me
Today I choose to see the gracious, merciful, and compassionate part of me
Today I choose to realize that the same understanding I extend to others I should extend to myself
Today I choose to provide the same time I give to another, to myself, and a little extra for good measure
Today I choose to extend the same mercy I provide to others to myself
Today I choose to intentionally give the same forgiveness I offer to others to myself
Today I choose to offer the same patience I extend to others to myself
Today the same love I give, exhibit, and shower on another, I am going to give, exhibit and shower on myself
Today I choose to see the liberties in me
Today I choose to see that the same way I believe in others, I must also believe in me
Today I choose to ensure that the same care I take with others, I am going to take with myself
Today I choose to offer the same encouragement I use to uplift another, to uplift myself
Today I choose to see that in the same way, I regard others, is the same way I must regard myself
Today the same way I choose them, I am going to choose me
Today I choose me because I deserve to be chosen
#ichooseme

Today I challenge you to write down some of the liberties you extend to others that you have not been extending to yourself? As you create your list, be sure to declare that you deserve those things from you as well. Remind yourself you are just as deserving of everything on your list.

TODAY I CHOOSE ME BECAUSE:

~Day 25~
Hello Blessed One

Psalm 37:4: "Take delight in the Lord, and he will give you the desires of your heart."
John 16:24: "Until now you have not asked for anything in my name. Ask and you will receive, and your joy will be complete."

There are times we ask for something but walk away before receiving it because deep down we do not believe we deserve it.

Today I choose me
Today I choose me because I deserve to be chosen
Today I choose to see the ask and receive in me
Today I choose to see how the ask + the receive in me will = the joy and happiness in me
Today because I choose me, I will ask for what I need
Today I will ask for what I want
Today because I choose me, I will go beyond the ask and boldly stand in a space of receiving
Today I choose to ask and receive all that I deserve
Today I choose to ask and receive all that life has to offer
Today I choose to ask and receive as my Father instructed
Today I choose to ask for _____ and wait on my Father to place it in front of me so I can receive it
Today I choose to no longer ask for what I want only to walk away before receiving it
Today I choose to see the ask and receive in me
Today I choose to see that if I do not ask, how can I receive
Today I choose to see that I have every right to ask, and even more right to receive
Today I choose to see that in my asking, I am choosing me
Today I choose to see that in my receiving, I am choosing me
Today I choose me because I deserve to be chosen
#ichooseme

Ask + Receive = Joy! I challenge you today to ask God to help you renew your mind and then receive it. What are some things you haven't asked for though you know you should? What are some things you have asked for but refused to receive? As you write your list ask God to help you to see that you can ask and receive.

TODAY I CHOOSE ME BECAUSE:

~Day 26~
Hello God's Likeness

Hebrews 12:1,2 (ESV): "Therefore, since we are surrounded by such a great cloud of witnesses, let us throw off everything that hinders and the sin that so easily entangles. And let us run with perseverance the race marked out for us, fixing our eyes on Jesus, the pioneer, and perfecter of faith."

Today I am unsure if I want to run the race. I am striving to persevere.

Today I choose me
Today I choose me because I deserve to be chosen
Today I choose to see the athlete in me
Today I choose to see the endurance I consistently display in this great race I am running
Today as I choose me, I will allow myself to run this race at the pace that I can and not at the pace that someone else has dictated for me
Today I choose to see that though I get tired, I will continue to consistently choose me
Today I recognize my choice of me will be reflected in how I choose others
Today I choose to see myself remove things that hinder me from running MY race
Today I choose to persevere beyond the hardships, obstacles, unexpected turns, and detours
Today as I choose me, I will listen to my body and rest when needed
Today I choose to get refueled, restored, and replenished on a consistent basis and not wait till I am forced to
Today I choose to see the strength in me as I ask for help when I need it
Today I choose me not because I must but because I want to
Today I choose to see I am equipped, prepared, and have been called to run MY race
Today I choose to see that no one can run MY race but me
Today I will not look left nor right to see how anyone else's race is being run
Today I choose to focus on me
Today I choose me because I deserve to be chosen
#ichooseme

Today I challenge you to answer this question. Have you been running your race for you or everyone else? Or are there just parts of your race that you consistently run for another over yourself?

TODAY I CHOOSE ME BECAUSE:

~Day 27~
Hello God's Daughter

Ecclesiastes 3:7 – "A time to tear, and a time to sew; a time to keep silence, and a time to speak;"

From the time I awaken to the time I fall asleep, I am constantly moving. I do not take the time to sit in silence. Nor do I take the time to repair myself.

Today I choose me
Today I choose me because I deserve to be chosen
Today I choose to see my silence and stillness
Today I choose to see that at times there is more power in my silence than in my words
Today I choose to see that in my silence I am saying, I do not need to fight this battle because this battle is the Lord's
Today I choose to see my stillness is so that God can do what I cannot
Today I choose to see that my silence and stillness is me sitting at His feet and being restored
Today I choose me in my silence
Today I choose to see that even in my silence I am still being heard
Today I choose to see that my silence is not a weakness but a strength
Today my silence allows me to listen
Today my silence allows me peace
Today my silence and stillness allow me to see if I am in fact choosing me
Today I choose to enjoy, embrace and relish in my silence and my stillness
Today I choose me
Today I choose me because I deserve to be chosen
#ichooseme

Is silence and stillness difficult for you? Why? What are some areas where you need to utilize your silence and stillness?

TODAY I CHOOSE ME BECAUSE:

~Day 28~
Hello My Sister in Christ

Proverbs 4:7 – "The beginning of wisdom is this: Get wisdom, and whatever you get, get insight."

I am in need of a realignment. I need to move wisely.

Today I choose me
Today I choose me because I deserve to be chosen
Today I choose to see what I place on the inside of me
Today I choose to ask myself
Does it feed me? Nourish me? Add value to me?
Today I choose to inquire of myself what am I taking in through
My ear gate?
My eye gate?
My mouth gate?
Today I choose whether I am willing to have it be a part of me forever?
Today I choose if it is worthy of taking up residence within me, even if only temporarily
Today I choose to see if what I place on the inside of me reflects me
Today I choose to inquire, does it add to me spiritually? Or does it drain me emotionally, mentally, physically, or spiritually?
Today I choose to see what I placed or allowed to be placed on the inside of me
Today I choose to see if what I placed on the inside of me is potentially dwelling with me and with Thee
Today I choose to see what no longer belongs within me
Today I choose to remove the things that no longer serve a purpose
Today I choose to remove things that have overstayed their welcome
Today I choose to revoke the lease that I have given to people and things that do not deserve it
Today I choose to see what will, from this point on, be placed on the inside of me
Today in choosing me, I choose to either remove, restore, adjust or rehab what is already there
Today onward as I continue to choose me, I will intentionally choose to add or deny entrance, or only take a portion of what is presented to place on the inside of me
Today I choose to see that I am to guard every part of me that allows something to enter me
Today I choose to see what I place or allow to be placed on the inside of me
Today I choose me because I deserve to be chosen
#ichooseme

Today I challenge you to make a list of things/people that either need to be removed, restored, adjusted, or rehabbed.

REMOVE (it's no longer serving a purpose, being used, not creating a space for what needs to be on the inside of me)

RESTORE (it needs to be repaired, rebuilt, it hasn't been used not because it isn't supposed to be but because as I grew, it didn't so once it's restored, it can be used again)

ADJUST (perhaps I have been using that thing for the wrong purpose or that person has been placed in the wrong space in my life)

REHAB (let go and let God, some things WE can't fix but God can so we let it go and get rehabbed and IF it comes back then and only then can it serve its purpose)

TODAY I CHOOSE ME BECAUSE:

~Day 29~
Hello Chosen One

Proverbs 31:10 (NKJV): "Who can find a virtuous wife (woman) ? For her worth is far above rubies."

This woman needs to be reminded that she has worth. This woman is me.

Today I choose me
Today I choose me because I deserve to be chosen
Today I choose the see the virtuous woman in me
Today I choose to see the helper in me; the partner in me; the integrity, discipline, and commitment in which I run my household
Today I choose to see the virtuous woman in me
Today I choose to see that if I make mistakes I can get back up and not allow them to consume me
Today I choose to see the virtuous woman in me is not about me saying I am perfect, but that in my imperfection I am more precious than jewels and my worth is far above rubies or pearls
Today I choose to feel comfort and encourage myself
Today I choose to use my mind and hands to work
Today I choose to consider all things before deciding to look after my friends and family, help those in need that cross my path, and care for myself
Today I choose to learn from my past and look forward to my future
Today I choose to be a thoughtful speaker and an intentional listener
Today I choose to be obedient to the Lord
Today I choose to see the virtuous woman in me
Today I choose me because I deserve to be chosen
#ichooseme

Today I challenge you to read Proverbs 31:10-31 and if you have never done it before, read it as if you are reading about yourself. Does it all resonate with you? What parts do you feel are talking about you and what parts don't you? Why?

Consider, being a virtuous woman is not about being perfect, it's about being intentional.

TODAY I CHOOSE ME BECAUSE:

~Day 30~
Hello Virtuous Woman

Philippians 4:8 (NKJV): *"Finally brethren, whatever things are true, whatever things are noble, whatever things are just, whatever things are pure, whatever things are lovely, whatever things are of good report, if there is any virtue and if there is anything praiseworthy - meditate on these things."*

Have I taken the time to meditate on why I am choosing me?

Today I choose me
Today I choose me because I deserve to be chosen
Today I choose:
My Eyes
My Ears
My Essence
My Energy
My Experience
My Everything
My Highs and Lows
My In-between
My Years of Circumcision of things that I have struggled with
My Years of harvest
My Years of lessons and my years of blessings
Today I choose me in all places and spaces
Today I choose me in the morning, and I choose me in the evening
Today I choose the past me, the present me, and the future me
Today I choose to spend my days living my life with the common thread that will be the choice of me
Today I choose to not end choosing me because it is day 30, but I will continue to choose me daily
Today I will choose me because every day I awaken is a declaration that I have already been chosen
Today I choose to date myself and pamper myself
Today I will fall in love with me if not for the first time, then I will fall in love with me all over again
Today I choose ME
Today and every day after today I will choose me because I deserve to be chosen
#ichooseme

I choose me today. I accept my virtue. I am making a proclamation that I will continue to choose me daily.

TODAY I CHOOSE ME BECAUSE:

notes to myself

- ○ Focus on choosing you
- ○ Be kind to your mind
- ○ Allow yourself joy
- ○ Do more of what you love
- ○ Do your own thing
- ○ Always be grateful
- ○ Create your own happiness
- ○

Daily Motivation

Choosing you means you are just as important as the people you choose everyday.

ABOUT THE AUTHOR

Lisa V. Taitt-Stevenson, a native New Yorker from Bed-Stuy, Brooklyn, made the decision to walk in her God-given purpose after over 20 years in Corporate America. This purpose ultimately would lead her to be a 6X published author, podcast creator, and host of Let's Talk Relationship not Religion, a platform that allows for the exploration of what a relationship with God can look like. As with any God-given purpose, living with intention is important and this has become the foundation of her Life and Relationship Coaching Services. These principals have paved the way for Lisa to become a Motivational Conversationalist and the development of LWI Publishing services. These things reflect her God-given desire to help people become the best version of themselves.
IG: authentic_author911

Made in the USA
Middletown, DE
12 March 2022

62382241R00073